TSUNAMI

Helping Each Other

BY

Ann Morris

&

Heidi Larson

M MILLBROOK PRESS   MINNEAPOLIS

The authors thank the following people who were helpful to them in the preparation of this book: Leanne Chadwick, parent representative, International School, Bangkok; Prasit Sathaporn Jaturawit, principal, Bang Sak School, Khao Lak; Boom Fitzgerald, translator; editorial assistants Elizabeth Losleben and Dena Gottesman.

Cover photographs courtesy of © Greg Huglin/SuperStock (wave);© Heidi Larson (left); © AP/Wide World Photos (right); Back cover photograph courtesy of © Heidi Larson

Photographs courtesy of © Heidi Larson: pp. 4, 6, 10 (right), 11, 12, 14 (left), 16, 17 (top right), 19 (top right, bottom right), 23 (left), 24 (top left), 26 (both), 27, 28 (all), 29 (all), 30 (all), 31; © CORBIS: p. 5; © OFF/AFP/Getty Images: p. 7 (both); © AP/Wide World Photos: pp. 8, 9, 10 (top left), 13 (bottom right), 21 (both), 23 (right), 24 (bottom left; top right), 25 (top left, top right; bottom right), 32; © Peter Parks/AFP/Getty Images: p. 10 (bottom left); © Paula Bronstein/Getty Images: pp. 13 (left), 17 (top left), 22 (bottom); © Andrew Wong/Getty Images: pp. 13 (top right), 17 (bottom), 18; © Johannes Simon/AFP/Getty Images: p. 14 (right); © Chris McGrath/Getty Images: pp. 14-15; © Pornchai Kittiwongsakul/AFP/Getty Images: p. 19 (left); © Roslan Rahman/AFP/Getty Images: p. 20; © Romeo Gacad/AFP/Getty Images: p. 22 (top); © Tim Graham Picture Library/Getty Images: p. 24 (bottom right); UNICEF/HQ05-0390/Palani Mohan/Thailand: p. 25 (bottom left).

Millbrook Press
A division of Lerner Publishing Group, Inc.
241 First Avenue North
Minneapolis, Minnesota 55401 U.S.A.

Website address: www.lernerbooks.com

Library of Congress Cataloging-in-Publication Data

Morris, Ann, 1930 –
Tsunami : helping each other / by Ann Morris and Heidi Larson.
        p. cm.
    isbn-13: 978-0-7613-9501-0 (lib. bdg. : alk. paper)
    isbn-10: 0-7613-9501-6 (lib. bdg. : alk. paper)
    1. Indian Ocean Tsunami, 2004--Juvenile literature. 2. Disaster relief--Thailand--Juvenile literature. I. Larson, Heidi. II. Title.
GC221.5.M67 2005
959.304´4--DC22   2005013616

Designed by Hans Teensma, Impress, Inc.

Manufactured in the United States of America
4 – DP – 5/1/10

AUTHORS' NOTE

When we first heard about the terrible destruction the tsunami had inflicted on many children and families in Southeast Asia, we wanted to write a book that would help children understand and remember this incredible event. It was our intention not only to depict the power of nature to destroy but also to help children see the courage of the people who live in this area and to know their responses to the event. In the course of researching and writing the story, we were particularly touched by the children's responses and the endlessly caring parents and teachers who brought them continued warmth and attention in the course of attending to their needs. It is our hope that children everywhere will be able to understand how, in the midst of this fiercest storm, with all its terrible turmoil, creating and learning, beauty and love, continue to prevail.

PUBLISHER'S NOTE

On January 3, 2005, I received a desperate e-mail from a friend in Japan. My friends Kayoko Yoneda and Cornelius Retting, who were thought to be in Thailand, were missing. A massive tsunami had hit Southeast Asia a week earlier, and neither Kayoko nor Cornelius had been heard from. Knowing how chaotic things might be in Thailand, I thought that perhaps they had just been unable to contact home. As the days passed, I learned that Kayoko and Cornelius had been overwhelmed by a fierce wave that had hit their hotel room in Khao Lak, Thailand, as they slept. Kayoko's body was found on January 11 and Cornelius's in April.

We were all affected by the devastating tsunami through the heart-wrenching media coverage. But the loss of Kayoko and Cornelius put this tragedy in very personal terms for us at Lerner Publishing Group. Kayoko, a picture book editor for Tokuma Shoten

Publisher Adam Lerner *(right)* with Kayoko Yoneda *(center)* and Cornelius Retting *(left)*

Publishers in Tokyo, worked at our company in Minneapolis in 1989 on a publishing exchange program. She was a unique person with natural curiosity and warmth. Cornelius was a respected publishing consultant in Germany. Both had a deep appreciation for nature's power. We are extremely proud to dedicate this book which, coincidentally, also takes place in Khao Lak, in memory of Kayoko and Cornelius. They will be dearly missed.

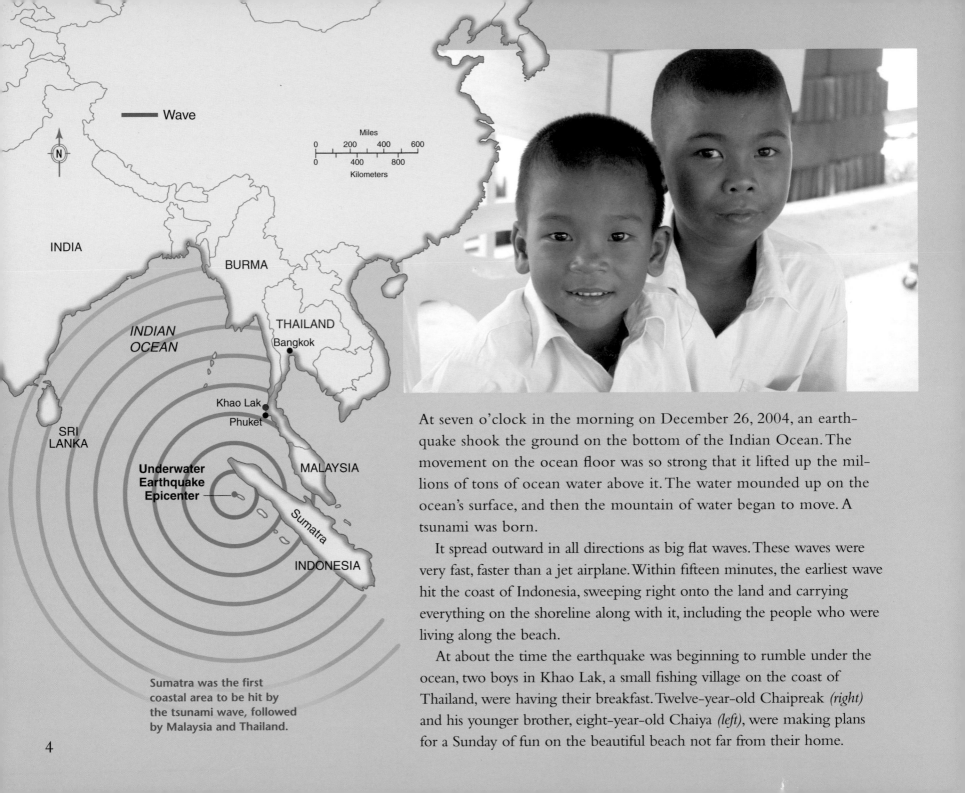

Wave

Miles
0   200   400   600

0   400   800
Kilometers

N

INDIA

BURMA

INDIAN
OCEAN

THAILAND
Bangkok

Khao Lak
Phuket

SRI
LANKA

**Underwater
Earthquake
Epicenter**

Sumatra

MALAYSIA

INDONESIA

Sumatra was the first
coastal area to be hit by
the tsunami wave, followed
by Malaysia and Thailand.

At seven o'clock in the morning on December 26, 2004, an earth-quake shook the ground on the bottom of the Indian Ocean. The movement on the ocean floor was so strong that it lifted up the millions of tons of ocean water above it. The water mounded up on the ocean's surface, and then the mountain of water began to move. A tsunami was born.

It spread outward in all directions as big flat waves. These waves were very fast, faster than a jet airplane. Within fifteen minutes, the earliest wave hit the coast of Indonesia, sweeping right onto the land and carrying everything on the shoreline along with it, including the people who were living along the beach.

At about the time the earthquake was beginning to rumble under the ocean, two boys in Khao Lak, a small fishing village on the coast of Thailand, were having their breakfast. Twelve-year-old Chaipreak *(right)* and his younger brother, eight-year-old Chaiya *(left)*, were making plans for a Sunday of fun on the beautiful beach not far from their home.

4

Fish abound in the waters around Khao Lak. The waters are known for black marlin (weighing up to 500 pounds) as well as sailfish, wahoo, several species of shark, and, more recently, shrimp and crabs.

The boys' parents had lived in the village of Khao Lak for several years and were pleased with the changes that had taken place there in the past decades. Although several of their friends and neighbors still earned their money from fishing, many more worked in the luxurious hotels that had sprung up along the beautiful coastline. Chaipreak and Chaiya's parents were both skilled stone-workers and had helped build several of the beautiful resorts that attracted tourists to their area. The money that their parents earned helped pay for the family's modest home.

The parents had a lot to do that Sunday morning. The boys' mother had to wash a week's worth of family laundry, while their father had to go into the beachside town to help a friend repair his motorcycle. And the boys were going off to the beach to meet their friends.

Of course, there was no way the parents could know about what had just happened under the ocean more than 800 miles away, so they happily saw the boys off for their morning of play on the beach. Then they each went out to begin their morning chores.

The glittering Khao Lak hotels attracted guests from around the world.

Chaiya and Chaipreak ran toward the ocean, chasing each other in and out of the trees. Nothing seemed unusual; it was very quiet. There were no animal sounds . . . but they began to hear an unusual roaring sound. And then they saw a huge wave coming right up out of the water and moving straight toward them. The boys were both good climbers, and Chaipreak yelled to Chaiya to get up into a tree! Chaipreak swiftly climbed to the very top of a palm tree, while his brother ran up a cashew tree nearby.

As the boys sat in the tops of the trees, the sound was deafening. When they looked down, they could not believe what they were seeing. The water swept underneath them, carrying everything in its path. Furniture, cars, boats, and even big chunks of houses swirled past them . . . and still the water kept coming!

They were not afraid. The trees felt sturdy beneath them. The water slowed at certain points, but their instincts told them not to come down yet. Just as the water slowed down, it started rushing again—this time back toward the ocean. The boys stayed in their trees for more than an hour, until everything seemed quiet below.

Of course the young boys did not take these pictures as they scampered up trees, but this scene is very close to what they saw. The actual photographs were taken by a British tourist, from the upper story of a hotel that was on the same beach, not far from where the boys were playing.

Boats that had been tied at piers along the beach were found inland, and cars were tossed about in the water as if they were toys.

When they came down, their feet sank into the mud, and it was difficult to walk in places as they headed toward their home. What they saw along the way frightened them. They saw injured people still clinging to trees or floating on bits of debris. Cars and even boats were every which way. Familiar sights had changed completely. Houses were not where they once were. When they reached the site where their house used to be, they saw nothing but a field of mud. Their house had been completely swept away along with those of their neighbors.

Their mother was waiting for them near where their house once stood. She was afraid that the tsunami would return. After hugging the boys and seeing that they were all right, she led them to the high ground of the mountains where the tsunami had not reached. That night, they slept on the mountainside. A cousin whose house was partway up the mountain brought them water and food and some clothes to keep them warm. After all they had been through, they were very thankful they had a dry and safe place to spend the night.

The tsunami wave swept away entire neighborhoods. The closer homes were to the beach, the more likely they were to be turned into piles of rubble. Many who fled to higher ground to escape the oncoming wave did not recognize their own neighborhoods when they returned.

In the morning, the boys and their mother set out in search of their father. They could not find him. This was a very sad time for Chaiya and Chaipreak.

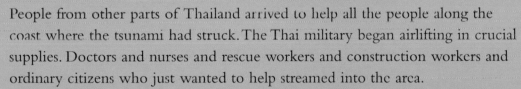

People from other parts of Thailand arrived to help all the people along the coast where the tsunami had struck. The Thai military began airlifting in crucial supplies. Doctors and nurses and rescue workers and construction workers and ordinary citizens who just wanted to help streamed into the area.

The first priority was to find the injured people. Those who were severely injured were airlifted out, while thousands with minor injuries were taken care of in makeshift first-aid centers along the beach.

The saddest task of all was to identify those bodies that had not been lost in the sea. The tsunami wave killed more than 5,300 people in Thailand, nearly half of them tourists visiting the area's seaside hotels. The others were local people who made their homes along the coast, such as Chaipreak and Chaiya's family. Another 2,900 people are still listed as missing.

Hopeful relatives often placed photographs of missing loved ones on top of the rubble where a family's home once stood.

On higher ground away from the beach, where houses had been knocked down but not obliterated, there were piles of house parts, household goods, and personal possessions everywhere. But when Chaipreak, Chaiya, and their mother returned to visit the site of their home, there was not even any rubble to sift through. They could not tell where their house had once stood.

The horrible mess and the loss of homes and possessions seemed to be unimportant to those who were still awaiting word about missing family and friends.

The tents gave people shelter from the hot sun and pouring rain for the first weeks after the tsunami.

The early rescue workers had brought tents with them. Entire neighborhoods that once had houses became tent cities, with each family crowding under their fragile shelter for protection at night.

As skilled workers began to arrive, they quickly built temporary shelters. Chaipreak, Chaiya, and their mother, along with many of their neighbors who had also lost their homes, moved into one of these structures.

Relief for the Thai tsunami victims
came in many forms. United
Nations secretary-general Kofi
Annan opened a world summit on
Asia's tsunami disaster with an
appeal for nearly a billion
dollars in immediate emergency
aid to tackle the aftermath
of the catastrophe.

Hundreds of people arrived
from many different countries
(the workers above are from the
United States and France), creating a worldwide community effort
to aid in rebuilding.

Chaiya enjoys a book at the relief
center that would be his family's
home for many months.

The boy in a relief center at right
sits in front of a mountain of
donated clothing and supplies
from citizens of many nations.

Most of the Buddhist monks lived in the hills, but they gave up their quarters so that bodies could be laid out there and identified. The monks came down to the villages to be with the grieving people and offer them comfort.

People arranged special food offerings for the monks as they prepared to pray for all of those villagers who had lost their lives. Mourners also left small Buddhist statues in those places where their loved ones were believed to have been when the tsunami hit.

Ritual food offerings in honor of the dead help the mourners deal with their sense of loss. The yellow-robed monks were a familiar sight on the streets of Khao Lak as people lined up to make their offerings in honor of their deceased and missing relatives.

The tourists who survived the tsunami left the stricken area by boat or plane, although many stayed for a time to become part of the volunteer cleanup squads. Almost all the hotels were decimated, and tourists stayed in the shelters along with local residents. Efforts are already well under way to rebuild the hotels and recover the thriving tourist industry of Khao Lak and nearby beach communities.

The tragedy affected not only the Thai coastal dwellers but also citizens from many other countries. The beautiful hotels, which Chaipreak and Chaiya's parents had helped to build, attracted vacationing families from all continents.

It was a beautiful Sunday morning, and many tourists were already out on the beach. Others were on the lower floors of the hotels, enjoying an ocean view over breakfast. The last thing they expected was an event that would affect their lives forever.

When the wave hit, many people were washed out to sea. Even months later, there are bulletin boards and display cases showing pictures of the missing tourists. Families are hopeful that they will still find some evidence of their missing relatives.

21

By far the most complex operation was the tracking of missing tourists. The hotels along the beach were full of vacationers for the week between Christmas and New Year's Day. Although some of the guests were from Thailand, the vast majority came from other places around the world. Soon people began arriving to search for missing relatives. Their hope was to be able to find their loved ones in a hospital, perhaps unable to communicate.

Hundreds of volunteers used computers to scan images into a centralized database for the benefit of those trying to find missing family members.

Alongside the cruise ships and helicopters and army transports, small craft helped transport food and water to the area as well.

The Thai government and international agencies led the relief efforts, but everyone helped. The local police missing persons' bureau worked to reunite families. Chaipreak and Chaiya and other younger children helped with cleanup work on the beach. And even animals joined the efforts, with elephants doing some of the heavier cleanup work and dogs participating in search-and-rescue operations.

As the Thai people began to rebuild their lives, the world came to help. National government and private agencies coordinated their efforts in support of the victims.

Clockwise from upper left: The Tsunami Volunteer Bureau coordinated the efforts of the people and organizations who arrived to bring aid; former presidents Bill Clinton and George H. W. Bush visited Thailand to offer their personal words of condolence on behalf of the United States and to help raise money for the relief effort; working on behalf of the Red Cross, Britain's princes William and Harry join volunteers to pack supplies for tsunami victims; the Brazilian air force prepares a load of humanitarian aid for Thailand.

Clockwise from upper left: Thai volunteers unload ration bags from a Thai navy helicopter; doctors from a Swiss humanitarian aid unit take inventory of emergency medical supplies; highly trained Japanese rescue workers search for tsunami victims; young students work with UNICEF, packing school supplies to be shipped to the stricken areas.

Life was never going to be the same for the residents of Khao Lak, but gradually some order was restored. The most joyous moment for Chaipreak and Chaiya was the day their school reopened. The Bang Sak School had been totally destroyed by the tsunami, and the Thai army and volunteers built them a temporary school.

Teachers brought clothes for children who had lost theirs during the tsunami. Special drinking-water tanks were provided to replace the broken water pipes in the area. Other schools in Thailand donated desks and school supplies.

After spending long days working on cleanup projects and thinking about what had happened to them, the boys now had somewhere to go each day. It felt good to be able to talk with their friends, many of whom had also lost loved ones in the tsunami. And, they were happy to start learning again.

The new school may have lacked walls, but to the students it was a beautiful building, a place that would add some structure to their post-tsunami lives.

The tsunami had made the soil in the entire area wet. The children had to remove mud from their shoes before going into the classroom.

Although Chaipreak and Chaiya were living in a shelter near the school, many of their friends had to travel long distances on mud-clogged roads in order to get there. The children who didn't live near the school were picked up by a school bus, while a few were brought to school by their parents on motorcycles. But, however they got there, the trip was well worth it.

The school day began with a hearty breakfast of porridge made from rice and meat, provided by one of the caring organizations. During breakfast they could talk with their friends and teachers. The children then happily helped wash dishes and sweep floors. Most of them had not done simple domestic chores since the tsunami, and these simple daily activities offered them comfort and security.

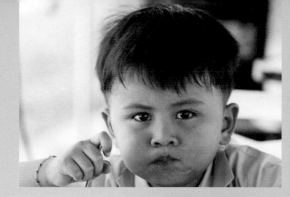

Life became more and more normal with each day. Soon they were opening their day with the traditional Thai greeting, the Swasdee, with their two hands together. And they also did their version of a pledge of allegiance, by holding up three fingers as a pledge to the king. All of these morning activities brought them together and made them feel connected to one another again.

Now the Thai army is at work on a brand new school building, right where the old one used to be. Every day the children watch from their temporary school as their new building grows. And, wonderful news for Chaipreak and Chaiya and their mother—they will soon be moving into a new home in their rebuilt neighborhood.

The help that the family received from people they had never met before has given them a sense of safety and security again. They will never forget the horrible fear of the tsunami. Their father and their friends and neighbors who did not survive the event will always be in their hearts, but now there is hope in their hearts as well.

Children's drawings of the tsunami are often frightening, especially compared to their charming pre-tsunami pictures of the ocean.

Thai schoolchildren look on as paper lanterns rise skyward during a ceremony to remember the tsunami victims. Light fills the sky, always a symbol of hope.

Barely five months after the tsunami waters receded, the International School Bangkok (ISB) Tsunami Relief Network had met its initial goal of raising $800,000 for a classroom building at the site of the former Bang Sak School in Khao Lak. As of August 2005, 716 students had enrolled in the new school, including 181 tsunami orphans. Construction on the dormitories began first so that the orphaned children would have permanent homes (now they are being cared for by members of the teaching staff and others in the community). In addition to the classroom building and dormitories, a computer center, an auditorium, a kitchen, a nursing station, a second classroom building, and a water tower are under way.

A portion of the proceeds from this book will be donated to the ISB Tsunami Relief Network. To track the progress of the effort or to donate funds, go to http://www.isb.ac.th/Content/Detail.asp?ID=1641.